T0146417

Also by Alan j. Wright

Media Starters
Cosmo's Cure
Quality Conversations in the Classroom
Reading Comprehension—Alan Wright et al.
Igniting Writing: When a Teacher Writes
Searching for Hen's Teeth: Poetry
from the Search Zone

I BET THERE'S NO BROCCOLI ON THE MOON

MORE POETRY FROM THE SEARCH ZONE

ALAN J. WRIGHT

BALBOA.
PRESS

A DIVISION OF HAY HOUSE

Balboa Press books may be ordered through booksellers or by contacting:

Balboa Press
A Division of Hay House
1663 Liberty Drive
Bloomington, IN 47403
www.balboapress.com.au
1 (877) 407-4847

Because of the dynamic nature of the Internet, any web addresses or
links contained in this book may have changed since publication and may
no longer be valid. The views expressed in this work are solely those
of the author and do not necessarily reflect the views of the publisher,
and the publisher hereby disclaims any responsibility for them.

The author of this book does not dispense medical advice or prescribe
the use of any technique as a form of treatment for physical, emotional,
or medical problems without the advice of a physician, either directly
or indirectly. The intent of the author is only to offer information
of a general nature to help you in your quest for emotional and
spiritual well-being. In the event you use any of the information in
this book for yourself, which is your constitutional right, the author
and the publisher assume no responsibility for your actions.

Any people depicted in stock imagery provided by Thinkstock are
models, and such images are being used for illustrative purposes only.
Certain stock imagery © Thinkstock.

Print information available on the last page.

ISBN: 978-1-5043-0517-4 (sc)
ISBN: 978-1-5043-0518-1 (e)

Balboa Press rev. date: 11/15/2016

For all those young poets who allow
the words to reach their hearts.

Poetry should be fun.
Fun in the head and fun on the lips!

Alan j. Wright, aka Alvin j. Riot, has been
writing poetry for this long and will continue
to seek inspiration in words and ideas.

Eye of Alan

Please note all photographs used in this
book were snapped by the author.

TABLE OF CONTENTS

THOUGHTS OF A POET

I spent a lot of time thinking about the title for this anthology of poems. Months, in fact. As a boy, I spent a lot of time admiring the moon. It was a mystery ball in the sky at night. So far away ...

Some years later, my first year as a teacher it turned out, a man named Neil Armstrong became the first person to set foot upon the moon's surface. It was a historic and an unforgettable event. So the moon deserves a special mention in the title.

Broccoli gets a mention for a whole other reason. Broccoli and I have been engaged in a battle for as long as I can remember. I didn't like it as a small boy, and I barely tolerate it as a grown-up. I know it's supposed to be good for me, but I am happy not to see it on my plate or find it trying to hide among other vegetables.

Broccoli and the moon together in the same title. Hope you can appreciate my thinking.

Alan J. Wright
Mornington
Victoria
Australia

Fair Whack

All the kids
Gathered in the park to play cricket.
Banger Barnes was batting—
Whack!
The ball exploded from the bat.
High in the sky it flew,
Above the trees,
Away into the dazzling sunlight;
Out of the park
And over the road.
It bounced beside Mrs. Bradford's cat, Boofhead and
Then bounced again
Before shattering Mr. Stravlakis's front window.
Over in the park, everyone froze.
Then ...
Scotty scampered,
Veronica vamoosed,
Davo decamped,
Skeeter skedaddled,
Abdul absconded,
Dominic dashed,
Betsy bolted,
Natalie nicked off,
Flynn flew the coop,
Wazza whisked to the woods,

And Banger Barnes hotfooted it home,
Like Speedy Gonzales yelling, "Arriba, Arriba! Ándale!"

When Mr. Stravlakis entered the park,
All the kids had split …
Game over
—stumps.

TILLY TAYLOR'S TANTRUM

Attention please, shoppers,
We have a meltdown in aisle 4,
Right beside the confectionery stand.
Young Tilly Taylor,
Age five and a quarter,
Is experiencing a throwdown.
Customers are advised to avoid this area.
Tilly's mother said, "No,
I repeat, no,
I will not add a packet of Jelly Snakes to the shopping
trolley."

And so
A throwdown is happening right here, right now.
We have—whaaa!
Piercing screams,
Yelling and spit.
Devil eyes,
Foot stomping,
And hate stares.
We have trolley rattling
And more.

Shoppers in aisle 4 are advised to move immediately
To alternative aisles.
Tilly's mother is moving towards frozen foods
In the hope of cooling things down.

Tilly Taylor remains in aisle 4,
Hollering and sobbing.

It appears we have a tantrum running out of steam
And scream.
Boohoo,
No Jelly Snakes today.
No way!

Thank you, shoppers, for your patience
In this crisis.

Price check on tissues.
Price check on tissues.

YESTERDAY

Yesterday,
I knew who my enemies were.
I knew where they lived.
I knew not to go there.
Yesterday, I knew where to play on the school ground
And that football was my favourite game in the whole
wide world.

Yesterday, I knew how disgusting it was to eat sheep
brains
And broccoli.
And oysters.
Yesterday, I could fly a kite,
Keep a secret,
And swing from the clothesline.
The world felt settled.

Then Laura Fisher spoke to me.

Now a million weird worries surround me,
And I'm not sure if I will survive grade 5.

I Quite Like that Stuff

Bees produce lots of it.
Carrots taste great when mixed with it.
Honey—
I quite like that stuff.

Recipes recommend it.
Trees produce it.
Olive oil—
I quite like that stuff.

Clouds deliver it.
Dams collect it.
Water—
I quite like that stuff.

Bodies grow it.
Hairdressers remove it.
Hair—
I quite like that stuff.

BEING A DANCER
(A POEM FOR TWO VOICES)

Being a dancer is a joy.
It's a disaster.
I'm a floating angel.
I'm a cannonball with lead wings.
When the music begins, I come alive to the beat!
When the music begins, I want to chew my legs off.
I'm elated.
I'm mortified.
My feet glide freely. I have the music in me!
My feet feel like jelly flippers. I only have muesli in me.
I am a twinkle-toed move'n'groover.
I'm a stinky-toed earth mover.
I feel simply wonderful.
I feel simply uncomfortable.
Watch me on the dance floor.
Poetry in motion.
I'm a storm out on the ocean.
I bump about.
I twist and shout.
I want to cry.
I want to fly.
On the dance floor I truly come alive.
I struggle to survive.
For me, dancing is syncopation.
Aggravation.
I've got the music in me.
Yo!
No!

ODE TO A TIE

You were the colourful one.
Draped across my shirt,
It was hard not to notice you.

In those days,
You went to school with me,
And your dazzling presence,
Your pattern of bright flowers,
Snapped eyes to attention.
You were a carpet of colour,
A glowing statement on an otherwise drab day.

You served me well.
That is why
You remain with me.
We are tied
Forever.

STARING AT BEARS

Young Claire Delaware likes to stare at the bears
Whenever she visits the zoo.
"It's perfectly fair," Claire will declare.
"They get to stare at me, too!"

So they sit there and stare at each other
Whenever Claire visits the zoo,
Till Pierre, the friendly zookeeper,
Feeds the bears at quarter past two.

MUDDLED MESSAGES

I'll give you some advice,
And I'll give it for free.
You'd be a fool to listen to me.

I gathered some wisdom.
I'll share it with you.
A little bit muddled,
But it's the best I can do.

In November, always remember:

An apple a day killed the cat.
A bird in the hand gathers no moss.
A stitch in time saves two in the bush.
If at first you don't succeed, carry a big stick.
Don't count your chickens until the fat lady sings.
He who laughs last never boils.
A watched pot never comes to those who wait.
Loose lips shouldn't throw stones.
While the cat's away, two heads are better than one.
People who live in glass houses spoil the broth.

IF I WENT SKATING

If I went skating,
I doubt that I'd glide.
I'd wobble and shake;
I'd slip, and I'd slide.
I'd land on the ice,
And I'd get soggy jeans.
I'd bump into skaters.
Embarrassing scenes!
With wobbly legs
And both my arms waving,
If I went skating,
I would surely need saving.
If I went skating,
I would quiver and quake
All round the rink
Like a slippery snake.

WHEN GOOP DROOPS

A blob of goop
Began to droop
Like juicy stew
Or gluggy glue.
It dangled downward,
Green and blue.
This viscous goop
Hung from the roof.
It dropped and plopped
On my friend Ruth.

WHERE DOES POETRY HIDE?

Poetry hides
In my father's chair,
In the spidery webs that dangle from the cellar walls,
In the hideous taste of Brussels sprouts,
In the smell of stinky cabbage water,
In a mother's gentle hands,
In a child's curious eyes,
In the shape of a stick insect,
In the morning song of magpies,
In the crash of waves pounding the beach.
Poetry hides here.

LEATHERCASE

It revolves in the small boy's fingers.
The ball spins in the air
Before he catches it yet again.
A cricket ball,
A four-piece leathercase.
Not a corky,
Not a compound ball;
Certainly not plastic.
This ball is the real deal.

Time and again
He watches it spin through the air—
Cherry-red leather,
White, raised seam.

He sits on the end of his bed
With dreams of bowling the perfect delivery—
Unplayable.
It spins from his fingers,
Floating above the batsmen's eyes,
Dipping suddenly
Before hitting the pitch with hiss and grip.
Eluding the probing bat,
Clipping the bails,
Breaking the wicket.
The perfect delivery
Is the boy's eternal summer dream.

It revolves in the small boy's fingers.
The ball spins in the air
Before he catches it yet again.
A cricket ball—
A four-piece leathercase.

MONDAY, MONDAY, NOT A FUN DAY

On Monday mornings, I feel morose.
I move my miserable muscles
Like a monkey with the measles.

On Monday mornings, I wish it was midnight.
I move like a mushy macaroon.
I am a mostly melancholy monster.

On Monday mornings, I am moderately mean,
A maddening monotone moaner.
Misery is my Monday morning master.

On Monday mornings,
I munch my muesli
And move miserably towards my school.

UNDERNEATH

Under the stars
There are the ingredients of creation
Gathered on a spinning sphere.
The dirt of eons.
Under the dirt are worms of the earth,
Night crawlers that cleanse the bones of the dead;
Bones of successive generations.
Under the bones lie the beginnings of time.

DOOVERLACKIE

When my dad fixes things
Around our house,
He sometimes asks me to help.
He calls me his apprentice.
He calls me his fetcher.
He calls himself Mr. Fixit.
He asks me to pass him the things he needs.
"Pass me the dooverlackie,"
Says Dad.
Dooverlackie?
"Yes, beside the whatchamacallit."
Whatchamacallit?
"Yes, under the thingamajig."
Thingamajig?
"That's right, I need to unscrew the doodad on the gizmo."
Oh.
So I hand him what I think might be the dooverlackie
And just hope I'm right.
"No," says Dad,
"That's a …
That's a doohickie.
I only use that when I'm fixing a thingamadoodle."

Dad ruffles my hair
And smiles.

WRITING TIME WITH MISS DUNGEON

In grade 5,
Our teacher, Miss Dungeon,
Would ask us to write.
She called it a composition.
She gave each of us a book,
A book she called
A composition book.

Every Thursday,
Straight after lunch,
Was composition time.
We all knew this because Miss Dungeon
Would stand in front of the class
And, using her very loud voice
That made the windows rattle,
Announce,
"Open your composition books!"

With pencils poised,
We would sit silently,
Waiting,
Waiting,
Anticipating
Until Miss Dungeon,
Standing at the front of the room,
Giant-like on a raised platform,

Looked over her spectacles and announced the weekly
writing topic—

"Autobiography of an ant.
Start writing now!"

No smile.
No frown.
"Start writing now!"

A few kids began writing.
Some stared out the window.
Some froze at their desks.
And the rest of us stared at the blank white page of our
composition book.
No one looked at Miss Dungeon.
No one dared to look at Miss Dungeon.

"You've got twenty minutes.
Start writing!"

The room fell silent.
Pencils scratched wobbly words.

Blank pages slowly filled with ant words.
Miss Dungeon prowled the room,
Gliding along the aisles between our desks like a shark;
A grey nurse shark.

Suddenly, the silence was shattered.

"Add more detail!
Add more detail!"
Miss Dungeon demanded,
Jabbing her finger,
Spearing the page,
Sharing her rage with a bewildered writer.
After twenty minutes, Miss Dungeon bellowed,
"Stop writing!
Close your books!
Pass them to the front!"

We put our pencils down.
We sigh with relief.
We stop thinking about ants.

She will return our ant stories
Covered in red ink
And a mark out of ten,
And we will all await the next topic
When next Thursday
We will do it all again.
Composition—
A new topic
Thrown our way by Miss Dungeon.

Clouds

Majestic wanderers
Rolling across the sky
You are indeed a wonder of the heavens
Let me lie on my back
In the cool grass
And pay you the attention
You deserve.

CAT'S GOT MY TONGUE

Woke up yesterday feeling under the weather
And noticed that the cat had my tongue.
We didn't see eye to eye on that at all.
I chased the cat all over the house,
But the way I was feeling, I couldn't catch a cold.
I didn't want to fly off the handle
And end up on a slow boat to China,
So I decided to lay down the law to that crazy cat.
But because it had my tongue, I had to hold my horses.
By now I was on pins and needles
And slowly going bananas.
But because I wasn't born yesterday,
I was determined not to put my head in the sand.
So, instead, I put my nose to the grindstone.
It was just what the doctor ordered.
I began to feel like a million dollars.
I cornered that cat in the kitchen.
That tongue-stealing tabby
Was sitting on the handle of the frypan
Like the cat that had swallowed the cream.
'Til finally it flew off the handle
And leapt from the frying pan into the fire.
I picked up my tongue
And couldn't do a thing wit thit.
I was left wondering, *Who let the cat out of the bag?*

KISS CHASEY

All the kids in the street
Gathered in Alan Prebble's
Front garden.
Bikes on the grass,
A gang of eight,
Milling around the shrubbery,
Talking,
Just talking.
Then someone said
We should do something.
Then there was silence
Until Barry, a big kid, said,
Let's play a game.
Then the muttering began.
A hubbub of mumbles and mutterings.
In the midst of the murmurs,
A voice rose up like a wisp of smoke,
A wisp of smoke from a country cottage chimney.
We could play kiss chasey, the voice whispered.

A pause ...
Then an okay was uttered.
Not too sure who said it
Or why.
I was only nine years old,
And I knew ...
Well, not much.
I certainly had never heard of kiss chasey.

The mention of the words "kiss chasey"
Made the girls squeal and the boys blush.

Barry explained the rules.
It's simple really, said Big Barry.
The girls run and hide.
The boys try to find them …
You've only got two minutes.
And, if you find one, you can give her a kiss
If she lets you.
Do you have to?
Asked Alan Prebble.
Well, the game *is* called kiss chasey.
Oh, yeah.
I suppose you're right, said Prebbs.

The girls scattered into the garden,
Still squealing.
The boys followed after counting to one hundred
Slowly and deliberately,
Like extras in a zombie movie.
I trailed behind,
A little bit confused.

Suddenly,
Ahead of me, I saw her,
Standing beside the hydrangea bushes
Like a statue.
Unmistakably, it was Margo,
Staring straight ahead,

Frozen in time.
Margo, the cool dream girl.
Margo, who made me nervous.
Margo, who made me feel awkward.
That Margo.

I slowed,
I glowed
As the distance between shrank.
Margo was still staring,
Barely blinking.
What was she thinking?

Knees shaking,
Heart racing,
I somehow took a hesitant step forward.
An invisible magnet drew me closer to dream girl Margo.

Contact!
A soft, dry kiss;
All over so quick.
No lip lock.
No lingering here.
I stepped away.
Away.
Away.
Now, it was me staring.

Margo slowly raised her arm
And dragged it across her mouth,
Removing the boy germs.

No words.
Just a look of disgust, spreading across her face
As if she'd been kissed by a frog.
A weird, warty, swampy frog.

She slowly wandered off,
Leaving me
Welded to the spot,
Staring at the hydrangea bushes.
Crestfallen—
The boy with wonky lips
And crumby kisses.
Frog boy.

Right there
In that moment,
I decided I would never play
Kiss chasey again.

ABBY CAT

A one-eared cat
Name of Abby
Had matted fur,
Particularly shabby.
Her teeth were sharp,
Her claws were grabby,
And she lurked in the shadows near Westminster Abbey.

CHEESE TO PLEASE YOU

An old man who lived in Kildare
Found a large purple mouse in his hair.
He named the mouse Milton
And fed it on Stilton,
Although it preferred Camembert.

MARY'S TOES

Mary's big toes were quite hairy,
And this amused her caged canary.
But the cows in the field
When her toes were revealed
Refused to enter the dairy.

WINDOW WONDERING

I stand
At the window, gazing,
And my thoughts fall upon important matters.
And I wonder ...
Does the window need cleaning?

RAW BEAUTY

Standing at the bus stop
On Vanderbilt Avenue,
Stick trees line the street;
Silent soldiers on a bleak avenue.

In a token shelter
Three women stand.
I huddle in my flimsy coat
Nearby.
An icy wind,
Rampant, raw
Slaps my face
With a bully's rage.

Above the wind
And the ugly song of the traffic,
I hear whistling.
Faint at first, yet familiar
Melodic carols
Carried higher than the street noise.
"Let heaven and angels sing!"

A man,
Thin and whiskery,
His winter cap at a jaunty angle,
Leans against a wall of grungy graffiti,
Whistling his selection of Christmas cheer.
Beauty in the raw,

Rising above the cacophony of cars and trucks.
Rising, rising
Until I hear only the whistling man.
His joyous carols a chorus for angels, kings, and commuters,
Soaring above the drabness of the day.
His lilting air
Lifts me from the ordinary.

I enter the bus
Determined to thank him.

And I do ...

I'VE NEVER WRITTEN ROTTEN

I'd like to be a writer.
A wizard with a story.
Maybe I could write a novel
Exciting, but not gory

Or maybe I write a poem
With words that make you weep.
A play about alien monsters
Who stomp about while you sleep.

Yes, I'd like to be a writer
With words that astound and amaze.
I could write of a million adventures,
And my life would have wonder-filled days.

I could write a report on hypnosis
Or the words for a rock moppet's song
Or a book to outsell *Harry Potter*
Or letters from downtown Hong Kong.

But at this stage I'm just a young author,
And writing improvement I seek.
So each day I'll practice my writing
Till my writing reaches a peak.

So if your writing sometimes looks sloppy,
Or you can't find your writing utensil,
Keep striving to make it outstanding,
And for goodness sake, don't chew your pencil.

Pets at School

Annabel entered the classroom,
And from her oversized backpack,
She took her lunch box,
Her take-home book,
And a cat!

Annabel didn't have any soft toys to bring to school.
Annabel didn't have a budgie in a cage.
All she had was a good idea.
A very good idea.
Annabel's idea.

I'll bring something to show my class.
I'll bring something special for show and tell.
Something very, very special.

On the way to school,
Annabel saw a cat, sitting on the lawn outside her
neighbour's house.
A cat sitting quietly on the lawn.
A small, purring, tortoise-shell kitty.
A cat just the right size to fit in a backpack.
So now we have a cat in our classroom.
A kitty cat.
A catnapped kitty cat.

Not exactly purrfect!

BACKYARD BLUES

Standing in the backyard,
Grumpy to the bone,
Slumped against the glum tree,
Miserable, alone.

Got those misery-makin',
Laughter-takin',
Low-down,
Backyard blues.

I've been grounded,
Compounded.
My friends are out runnin',
Funnin',
While I'm slumped against the glum tree,
Grumpy to the bone.

Got those sad-makin',
Smile-shakin',
Low-down,
Backyard blues.

I'm dejected,
Suspected,
Terminally affected,
Totally disconnected.
Still slumped against the glum tree,
Still grumpy to the bone.

With those no bike ridin',
Five day no playin',
Low-down,
Backyard blues.

BORED

I'm bored.

Horse yawning,
Eye blinking,
Time dragging,
Sleep craving,
Foot twitching,
Sigh heaving,
Brain bulging,
Fly watching,
Freckle counting,
Fun fading,
Hope sinking,

Bored.

EMBARRASSED

I'm embarrassed.

Pants wetting,
Cheek burning,
Step tripping,
Food spilling,
Banana slipping,
Mom dancing,
Dad singing,
Dog farting,

Embarrassed.

ODE TO FLUFF

Oh, amazing fluff.
Light and airy.
Soft and hairy.
You gather in corners
And snuggle in navels.
What is your purpose?

Oh, amazing fluff.
I feel you in my pockets,
Nestled in the deepest corners,
Tangled and spongy,
A little bit grungy.

Oh, amazing fluff,
With your hint of lint,
You are lightweight stuff.
But that's
Apparently enough!

IMAGINE

Imagine a pig in a bright purple wig.
Imagine a duck, driving a truck.
Imagine a cow, pushing a plough.
Imagine a hen that can count up to ten.
Imagine a sheep that can't go to sleep.
Imagine a goat, wearing a coat.
Imagine a horse with a bottle of sauce.

When we go to the farm, we won't see them, of course.
But …

Just imagine!

I'm Talking Excited!

I'm talking excited.
I'm talking bounce.
I'm talking hubbub,
Flurry, and flounce.

I'm talking elated.
I'm talking ado,
Ferment, and fever.
It's a hullabaloo.

I'm talking commotion.
I'm talking feeling,
Disturbance, and drama.
I'm talking *squealing.*

I'm talking hysterics.
It's such a to-do.
I'm talking *excited*!
How about you?

Not Fantastic

My neighbours below have a ceiling fan
That rotates all through the night.
And I am but a prisoner
Of its droning circle of flight.

A whirling, twirling turbine,
It drums and thrums in my brain.
It sucks the sleep from my night of rest.
I toss and turn in pain.

Spinning, just spinning forever,
An endless droning throng.
I wish that it would cease
Its maddening, monotone song.

That fan keeps rotating,
Relentless pulsating,
Drilling deeper into my head.
And I lie there, waiting,
Just longing for silence,
Trapped in a nightmare I dread.

The throbbing of those blades
Has created a tormented man.
I feel like I'm a movie star
Constantly stalked by a fan.

I ain't no fan of that fan, man.

Rainforest Rage

Industrial societies
See forests as needless woods,
Occupying land,
Getting in the way of development.

Every second the planet loses another two football fields
Of its precious rainforest cloak.

A picture
I could not conceive ...

An earth without forests.

We are the cause of deforestation.
We create widespread destruction.
We clear away the future.

Ripping and tearing,
Burning,
Destroying.

We devastate.
Humans remain a cancer suffered by the lungs of the
earth.

Keep Away from Cliff Edges

I read a sign that told me to keep away from
Cliff Edges
Problem is …
I've never met him.
So I don't really know what he looks like,
And that's a problem.

How do I keep away from someone I can't even recognize?

I could be standing next to Cliff Edges at the bus stop,
And I wouldn't know it.
I could be sitting next to Cliff Edges at the beach,
And I wouldn't know it.
I could be flying in a hot air balloon with Cliff Edges,
And I wouldn't know it.

I wonder about Cliff Edges.
Is he a scallywag—as my nana calls some boys?
Or is he something worse?
Maybe Cliff Edges is a ratbag?
A nincompoop?
A bully?
Maybe he's just a little misunderstood—as my mum likes to say.

I will keep my eyes open
Just in case
I run into him,
This most mysterious character—
Cliff Edges.

School Bag and Banana

At the bottom of a cupboard
I discovered my old school bag.
It no longer had my lunch in it.
My school jumper was missing,
And no pencils could I find.
And though many years had passed
Since it had entered the school gate on my back,
I could still smell traces of banana
Trapped in its leathery hide.
Banana boy
With a schoolboy's lunch.
And for a moment I thought I heard the school ground
And its bittersweet call to come and play.

Martina Gets the Munchies

Martina was an astronaut
Aboard a rocket ship,
Hurtling through the galaxy,
Eating salt and vinegar chips.
She viewed the world from outer space;
Saw meteors whiz past her face.
And throughout her intergalactic trips,
She munched away on tasty chips.
Imagine what a time she faced,
All weightless in that far-out place,
Zipping swiftly through the sky,
Her favourite munchies floating by.

RED DOG IN LA-LA LAND

Red dog in La-La Land
Sounds silly,
Looks grand,
Strutting across the burning sand.
Red dog in La-La Land.

Red dog in boxer shorts.
Four shoes,
Odd sorts,
Sniffs twice,
Then snorts.
Red dog in boxer shorts.

Red dog with a curly tail
Lifts his leg
On a garden snail.
Sniffs the grass
To find the trail.
Red dog with a curly tail.

Red dog somewhat loopy
Chases shadows,
Looks quite droopy.
Crazy dog,
Not like Snoopy.
Red dog, somewhat loopy.

Red dog in La-La Land
Drinks ditch water,
Rolls in sand,
Chases tail,
Licks a hand.
Red dog in La-La Land.

CISCO, THE SMELLY ALLEY CAT

Cisco was an alley cat,
And a rather ugly one at that.
All scratch and bite, snarl and hiss;
A friendly cat would not do this.

Cisco didn't play nice.
Cisco didn't purr.
He stunk like rotten fish heads.
He was missing chunks of fur.

But not much worried Cisco.
He was king of all the cats.
He made the mice feel nervous,
And he scared away the rats.

Luigi owned a café
On the corner, near the alley.
He knew the cat was snarly.
He knew the cat was smelly.

But he threw him tasty morsels
Every single day.
He loved the work that Cisco did,
Keeping rats at bay.

HOMEWORK HAUNTS HAMLET

To do or not to do?
That is the question.

Whether 'tis nobler on the mind
To suffer the slings and arrows of outraged parents
and teachers
And engage willingly in work avoidance,
To look away from homework
And towards fun and merriment.

To do or not to do?
That is the question.

MY PEN

My pen leaks words,
Both sharp
And sweet.

Splinters
And honey.

Winter through the Window

The rain pelts
down
Wind rips and
roars
Compelling folk to
live indoors
Winter days
reign supreme
Summertime's a
distant dream
AJW

On Being Grounded

In my room,
On the very edge of doom,
I can't hear the dust settle on the bookshelves.
I can't see the curtains fading.
I can't feel the light coming through the window.
I can't touch the time that passes.
I can't smell the boredom
That grows steadily around me.

I'm grounded.
And things are happening around me
As I lie here
On my prison bed.
There are things over which
I have no control.

Being grounded
Has me confounded.

These have been the longest five minutes in history.
And why?
Well, it's a mystery.

WINDOW DRESSING

In the window of a shop
A dress
With polka dots and gaudy flowers,
Ribbons and lace
Is admired for a moment.

I would like to try it on,
The admirer announces.

A look in the mirror
Brings disapproving thoughts.
Doubt arises.
The salesperson brings reassurance.

Glamour,
Allure,
Admiration, and envy
Will be yours with this gown.

These flattering words
Work their magic.
Doubt vanishes.

The buyer twirls,
The dress swirls.
A smiling face is shrouded by curls.

I will buy the dress.
I will wear it now.
Consider this dress sold.

A MOMENT OF MOONY MADNESS

Sometimes,
Just for a millisecond,
A minispeck in time,
I feel wonderfully weird,
Moderately mad,
Conveniently crazy.
I am a full moon loon.

You see me
Camouflaged as a sensible soul.
A rational dude,
A fellow, generally mellow.

But I can whoop and holler
And leap over shadows,
And whistle loony tunes.
Like an utter nutter,
I can leave the sane lane.

I am warmed by my own wackiness.
I am unharnessed,
Unhinged,
Exuberant
Just for a millisecond,
A minispeck in time.

Then I resume normal transmission.

I Am a Shoe

I am a shoe.
A vehicle for your feet.
I am ready to take you anywhere you choose to go.
I am a shoe.
You may call me sandal.
You may call me boot.
You may call me slipper.
I am comfortable with these names.
I have you covered.

I am a shoe.
I can shuffle.
I can clomp and stomp.
I can dance until dawn.
I am a shoe.
Slip into my welcoming shape,
And tell me where to go.

I am a shoe.
I can live with smelly socks and stinky toes.
I can cope with you stepping on the squelchy, stinky
things of this world.

I may have a tongue,
But, fortunately, I have no nose.

Bully for Me

We had a bully at our school;
I think every school has one.
But ours left.
Now I can ride to school
Relaxed.

We had a bully at our school,
But ours left.
And now playtime is fun again.

We had a bully at our school,
But ours left.
I wonder if that person is happy
Like me and my friends
Are now.

Searching the Night Sky for Sputnik

Sputnik.
Say it quickly;
Sounds like a wet sneeze,
Dog slobber wet.
Sputnik,
World's first-ever satellite,
Launched from Russia
In the year 1957.
Circling the earth,
Racing through outer space,
Visible in the night sky.

A small boy
In striped, flannelette pyjamas
Stands in his front yard
On a cool October evening,
Staring up into the night sky,
Eyes searching the faraway spaces
For a moving light.
The light of Sputnik.
And suddenly he sees it.
The flashing light of the satellite,
Orbiting the earth.
A man-made wonder,
Zooming across the night sky
Above his front yard.
Sputnik—
Sounds like a wet sneeze
If you say it quickly.

TELLING TALES

I like to tell myself stories.
I invent them in my head;
They rock and roll around my mind.
They entertain me on the bus.
They are with me as I walk down Union Street.
They are there when I enter the subway.
They ride with me through the underground tunnels.
My stories roll around in my head until they are ready
to be told.

Then ...
They emerge
Like warm clothes from a tumble dryer.
Fresh, new,
And ready to be written
Across the pages of my notebook.

In my world,
It seems everything's write.

SOCK IT TO ME

When I was a little kid,
Knee-high to a grasshopper,
Grown-ups would say,
Pull up your socks, young fellow.
I'd look at my bare feet.
Then I'd look up again
And think,
Grown-ups are weird ...
Blind Freddy can see
I'm not wearing any socks,
So how can I pull them up?

CHANGES

I used to be an apple, but now I'm just juice.
I used to be a reason, but now I'm an excuse.
I used to be an eagle, but now I'm a feather.
I used to be a cow, but now I'm just leather.
I used to be a note, but now I'm a song.
I used to be a chime, but now I'm a gong.
I used to be a diamond, but now I'm a ring.
I used to be a rope, but now I'm a string.
I used to be a mountain, but now I'm a hill.

Finally, I'm a whale, just eating krill.

NOBODY LISTENS TO ME

My mother said,
That's nice, dear.
But, alas, I fear
On this occasion, she failed to hear.

My father said,
I'm busy right now.
He was staring out the window,
So I don't know how.

My brother was absorbed with this and that,
And my sister was distracted, feeding her cat.

Nobody listened to the words I said.
I may as well have a pineapple head.

So nobody listened.
No one can see
That a large, hairy monster
Is following me.

VITRIOL

Anger,
Vengeance,
Violence,
Rage;
Viper words scratched on a page.

SPOOKY

Weird,
Bizarre,
Scary thing;
Any book by Stephen King.

CHOOK LOOK

We're going to the farm today.
We're off to see the chooks.
We need some eggs for breakfast.
Let's give the chooks a look.
The roosters crow,
The chicks cheep,
The hens go cluck
While scratching deep.
I find an egg upon the ground,
Lying there all smooth and round.
In my basket I will place it
For if it breaks, I can't replace it.
Finding eggs is quite a pleasure,
Each one a tiny chooky treasure.

A COLLECTION OF
NURSERY CRIMES

Mary, Mary had a canary.
She kept it in a cage.
But when she fed it pizza,
It flew into a rage.

Little Boy Blue, stop blowing your horn.
Its monotone note
Has made me feel forlorn.
The sheep in the meadow,
The cows in the corn
Have all had enough
Of your loud, honking horn,

Hickory, dickory dock,
Three mice ran up a clock,
The clock struck one.
But the other two escaped uninjured.

Humpty Dumpty sat on a wall;
Humpty Dumpty had a great fall.
All the king's horses and all the king's men—
Just left him there.

CERTAIN SERIOUS SITUATIONS

Finding yourself in a seafood restaurant when you don't
eat fish
Is rather concerning.

Realizing you are on the wrong bus, going in the wrong
direction,
Can give you conniptions.

When you're searching for a light switch in the dark and
your hand touches something slimy,
Is just a bit scary.

When the door snaps shut behind you before you have
finished checking to see if you have your keys in your
pocket
Is very alarming.

Discovering you have an extra day to complete your
homework …
Absolutely priceless.

Follow Me

A father walks in the damp sand
Close to the shoreline.
His young son follows him closely.
The boy stretches to place his feet
Within his father's huge footprints.
The boy strives to match the man he so admires.
Follow my lead.
Walk this way.
The father shows the way forward,
And the boy willingly rises to the challenge.

Clear the Sandcastles Away

The beach is not a place to work hard.
Too hot and damp
And soft.
Never a place to conjure up fanciful dreams.
It rises against ideas,
Washing away thoughts and grand plans.

Rhythms of the sea capture our attention.
Waves
Slap the shoreline endlessly.
Wind
Dashes through the trees beyond the scrubby headland.
The slow flapping of a seagull skimming the surface of
the bay steals our gaze.

Under the spell of beach scenes
We relax,
We stretch.
Our thoughts flatten,
Leaving our minds bare and open.

Just as the tide washes away yesterday's sandcastles,
The ragged edges of our minds are gently smoothed
like sea glass.

HOLD YOUR HORSES

A bicycle with a flat tyre,
The world turning,
A game of Scrabble,
The breathing of a sleeping baby,
Grandma with a sore back,
Tortoises,
Tractors in a boggy paddock,
Teenagers waking up,
Snails,
Old computers,
Grey Monday mornings,
Sitting in the medical room,
Breakfast on a Sunday,
Honey oozing from a spoon.

All slow.
Oh, so slow.
Oh, so very s-l-o-w.

ANGER

I am one letter away from danger.
A bubbling cauldron.
I am an imminent eruption.
A frightening proposition.
I am an outburst of pent-up frustration.
Rebellion on the rise.
I am a spitting, sputtering fuse,
Close to exploding.
Steer clear.
Don't come near.
I am, without doubt, frightening.
A rod of lightning.

And my sister knows why.

LOTS OF LUNES

Think of me,
Diving gracefully into the lake,
Wearing pink slippers.

It is true.
I ate your peppermint slice.
It tasted disgusting.

In the morning,
I will cease snoring loudly
And startle everyone.

On the beach,
Lying languidly on a towel,
I sang opera.

I sat alone,
Watching a very scary movie,
Wearing a blindfold.

I Am Such Things and More

I am the leaf, clinging tenaciously to the tree as winter approaches;
The claw of the eagle, holding fast to its prey.
I am the wind, rustling the gum trees.
I am the cool breeze at the end of a summer's day,
The cackle of the kookaburra,
Laughter floating on the air,
A smile spreading slowly across your face.
I am in the thunderous crush of breaking waves.
I am lightning, illuminating the night sky;
The quivering tail of a mad dog,
The thud of an axe, slicing through a defiant log.
I am the patch of sun in the corner of the yard where butterflies dry their wings and lizards laze on rocks.
I am the heart of the matter.
I am the road, winding into the distance;
The wilderness track few have travelled.
I am the song of the magpie, rejoicing in each new morning.
The crunchy celery stem, and the bubbles in a glass of mineral water.
I am a delicate orchid, a hardy oak.
I am a plastic container filled with treats.
I am the scorpion when aroused.
I am a puddle of unknown depth.
The kite on the breeze.

I am the wondrous words that flow from a new pen.
I am the words in a book you can't put down.
I am a comfortable sock.
I am as firm as new boots.
I am the sun on your back.
Look for me in such things.

PREHISTORIC PREDATOR

He glides through the murky water,
Eyes snap-locked on his prey.
Silent assassin,
Waiting for strike time.
Waiting,
Waiting
For that certain moment.

He pounces.
The water churns.
Blood in his nostrils,
Teeth in his prey,
Death rolling fury
Away,
Away.

The victim drowns.
The monster dines
Before gliding away.
Ancient reptile,
Calculating
Crocodile.

A SMILE SO WORTHWHILE

You,
My friend,
Make me smile.
As do …

The cackle of a kookaburra,
Autumn sun on my shoulder,
Loud burps from little people,
A clean car,
Ice cream in summer,
Rain on the roof at night,
The thought of visiting Venice,
Planning my next holiday,
Watching my enemy trip up,
Cappuccino froth on someone's lip,
Rhubarb and apple pie,
Giggles,
Heartfelt hugs,
A large bunch of balloons.

Not a blister on my heel.

LEAF

It clung tenaciously
To its sturdy host.

Eventually the wind
Separated them,
And the leaf,
Cast adrift,
Began its inevitable descent.

Flittering,
Fluttering,
Falling
To earth.
A feather tumbling
Before landing
On the pathway
Face up.

Autumn shades exposed;
Brilliant at the end.
Intense hues of magenta, indigo, and russet red
Among the verdant green remnants.
Death-defying beauty.

PENNY PALMER'S PINK PYJAMAS

Penny Palmer's pink pyjamas
Were drying on the line,
Held in place by giant pegs.
Their pinkness, so divine.

A substantial woman was Penny P.
Her pyjamas quite immense.
They covered her from head to toe,
Which all made perfect sense.

The morning breeze began to grow.
It formed into a gale.
Those huge pyjamas on the line,
Flipped and flopped and flailed.

Penny Palmer's pink pyjamas
Lifted upwards in a flash.
Above her house they floated,
Gaudy and pink and brash.

The neighbourhood was puzzled
By pyjamas in the sky.
A sunset in the morning
Had sent the day awry.

Like floating blimps, the top and tail
Began drifting into space.
Tumbling pink pyjamas,
Disappearing without trace.

Penny P. stood by her gate,
A ciggy in her paw.
She knew she'd never wear
Those pink pyjamas anymore.

Penny Palmer's pink pyjamas
Were last sighted floating east
And ended up in Africa,
Beside a wildebeest.

CEREAL KILLER

It's Saturday morning.
I'm awake,
And, therefore, I'm hungry.
I shuffle to the pantry.
I stare.
The shelf is bare;
There's nothing there.
I'm old Mother Hubbard
Once more at the cupboard.
I have a bowl,
A spoon,
Milk,
And there's not a sign of Wheat Bix.
No packet,
No crumb.
I'm crestfallen, glum.
Somewhere out there
Lurks a cereal killer.

I'm ravenous.
My stomach, cavernous.
I'm *starvin'* Marvin.
This is immense.
It has me intense.
It's a big deal,
Earth-shattering.
Well, maybe not earth-shattering,
But it's enough to set me on fire.

It raises my ire.
I begin to perspire.
I'm miffed.
I've been stiffed.
My world's coming adrift.

Make yourself some toast, says Dad.
Have an egg instead, says Mum.
Suffer, hisses my sister the snake.
Make some porridge,
Suggests dear old Nan ...
Porridge?
It's summertime;
Surely I would melt.

Dad flops some money
On the table.
Ride to the shop,
And buy some more.
No big deal, my boy.
I just fume.

I'm desperate,
So I'm off on my bike.
An angry, anxious pedaler.

Halfway there
I realize something really important—
I'm still wearing my pyjamas.

I keep pedalling
On a mission
To the milk bar at the corner.
Breakfast cereal or break.

Mr. Nguyen,
Mr. Nguyen,
Have you got a packet of Wheat Bix?
Sorry, says Mr. Nguyen,
I'm all out of Wheat Bix.
Do you want Rice Pops instead?

I could scream.
I could cry
And yell at the sky.
I just want my Wheat Bix.
I just want my Wheat Bix.
I just want …
Mr. Nguyen says, try the supermarket.

Pedal, pedal, pedal
To the supermarket.
Hot, bothered, and famished,
I race down the cereal aisle
And snatch a super-size pack
Of the one and only
Wheat Bix; yeah!
Breakfast, here I come.

Pedal, pedal, pedal
Back home.
Dad's got his hand out,
Waiting for the change.

I'm hollow.
I'm empty.
I'm dog hungry, starving.
It's time to chow down.
Breakfast at last!

Munching and crunching,
No time for talking.
Cereal killers,
You will never beat me.

MY FLASH BIKE

I once owned a bicycle
So fine.
All mine;
A Healing Semi Racer,
With Semi Racer handle bars.

It looked flash.
It looked sporty.
Its silver frame shone in the sunlight.
The spokes glistened.
The wheels whirred.
Everything blurred.

When I charged down the street,
A tailwind at my back,
Atop my speedy machine,
Old ladies,
Dogs,
And rubbish bins
Were in peril.

When I went pedaling by,
Wheels whirring wildly,
The spokes glistened,
The wheels whirred,
Everything blurred.

TODAY

Today, I won't pull up my socks
Or improve my attitude.
Today, I will not volunteer to help.
Today, I won't put my best foot forward,
Nor will I rush to get somewhere.
I won't raise my hand and contribute to class discussions.
And today I won't be striving to do my best at all times.

Today, I think I may well
Scratch my ear with a pencil,
Stare out the window,
Pretend to read,
And watch a fly annoy Nina Pastucci.

Today, I feel slower than a slug in sludge.

Today, I am tired.
Today, I am floppy and droppy
And down in the dumps.

Tomorrow, who knows?

WINDOW

The important thing about windows is that they let in the light.

They fog up in winter.
They let the sunshine in.
They provide a view of the outside world.
And when they open, fresh air flows in.

But the important thing about windows is that they let in the light.

NAME-DROPPER

My dad knows lots of people,
I reckon.
He often tells me, Bob's your uncle,
But I don't know any Bobs.

He believes Scott is great.
He's always saying,
Great Scott!
He wants to rob Peter to pay Paul, and I'm not sure why.
He thinks Fanny Adams is sweet,
And someone called Nelly is nervous.
He tells me Larry is happy.
That's great, but I don't know Larry.
Last week he told me to run like Billy O.
How does Billy O run?
That's what I want to know.

Dad does a lot of things for a fellow called Pete Sake,
And he thinks Alec is smart because he's always saying
What a smart Alec he is.
He thinks Ann is raggedy,
And Simon is simple.
Freddie is blind,
But even he can see,
Which I find a bit confusing.

And somehow Johnny is on the spot.
And Jack is in a box.
Maybe it's the same box Pandora has,
And Dad often says he doesn't want to open that one,
Which I find a bit confusing.

So do my mates
Tom, Dick, and Harry.

SUMMER IN THE HILLS

In the summer
Of my hillside hometown,
I scampered up ladders to pick cherries.
I crouched on my haunches, gathering strawberries.
I ate nectarines straight from the tree
And fished for yabbies and native blackfish in the creek.
Under the shade of an oak tree I read *Prisoner of Zenda,*
While the chirping of crickets stole silence from the dusk,
And dragonflies hovered in the garden.
In the summer
Of my hillside hometown,
Heat haze shimmered over dusty red roads.
Flies moved without urgency,
And homemade ice-cream vanished in a lick.
Lemon cordial and ice blocks quenched our lingering thirst.
And as the air grew sticky in the late afternoon melting time,
Lemon-scented gumtrees left reminders on the breeze.
Dandelion lawns browned before our eyes,
And water tanks ran dry when the February dragon came calling.
We sought the shade of forest canopy,
Rode our bikes close to sunset,
And our eyes scanned the horizon for smoke.

Occasionally, we caught the bus to the Belgrave baths,
Along slow and winding roads,
And returned with chlorine-saturated towels.
No surfboards,
No seaweed,
No sand.
The coast and its waves were alien.
No Cowabunga.
No Gidget and Moondoggie.
And though we listened to the Beach Boys sing the praises of Barbara Ann
And danced the Stomp,
We lived in the valleys and on the ridges,
And we saw summer through a forest of ferns.
It was the same season,
Just dressed in a different outfit.

OH TO BE A PIRATE BOLD

Oh to be a pirate wild,
sailing the briny seas
With doubloons in my treasure chest
And shouting *Arrh* whenever I please.

Oh to be a pirate wild,
with a parrot on my shoulder.
I'd sailed to faraway islands.
No pirate would be bolder.

Oh to be a pirate wild,
with the crow's nest overhead.
No wooden leg, no eyepatch,
but a large black hat instead.

Oh to be a pirate wild,
and say, Shiver me timbers, all day.
Skull and crossbones full on view,
swashbuckling away.

Oh to be a pirate wild.
A buccaneer, courageous.
Breathing in the salty air,
a life somewhat outrageous.

MOLLY MURPHY'S MONKEY

Molly Murphy's monkey
Got a little bit drunk.
He
Fell out of a tree
And landed *ker-plunk.*
He
Picked up a banana
And ate a huge chunk.
He
Then fell asleep on Molly Murphy's bunk.
He
Woke up sad, and his spirits had sunk.
He
Promised to be good, and he never would flunk.
He
Needed a bath 'cause he smelled like a skunk.
He
Was Molly Murphy's

Drunky,

Hunky,

Chunky,

Flunky,

Skunky,

Monkey.

Raining in Rome

It's raining in Rome.
The morning sky,
The colour of a seagull's wing,
Glooms above us.
Thunder mumbles
Like a brooding
Teenager
Demanding attention.

Wandering

I wandered
Lonely as a clod.
Then noticed that my shoes were odd.
People passing in the street
Kept laughing
At my unmatched feet.

THE WORLD IS FULL OF SILLY SONGS

They say
Pop music is getting dumber.
That it's written for eight-year-olds.
It's simple.
It's dumb.
Syrupy rhymes and grammar crimes,
Don't-cha know.
Lame lyrics,
Sound bubbles blown out,
Boring and bland.

Well, I'm not a kid anymore,
But I remember,
"Yummy, yummy, yummy I've got love in my tummy."
And I remember,
"Someone left the cake out in the rain, and I don't think
that I can take it."
And I remember,
"My girl Lollipop, she makes my heart go giddy-up."

Lame lyrics are not new;
They criss-cross time.
These terrible tunes
Get stuck in our heads.
Earworms bore into our brains,
Snippets of irritating pop songs
On an endless loop

Like mosquitoes buzzing,
Like sirens wailing,
Like cats screaming.
Round and round they go,
Up and down they go,
Bopping around in the brain.

They say
Pop music is getting dumber.
That it's written for eight-year-olds.
It's simple.
It's dumb.
Syrupy rhymes and grammar crimes,
Don't-cha know.

Well, that's pop music.
It's got sugar sprinkled through it.
Saccharine sweet,
On repeat.
"But that's the way my mama, mama likes it."

CUSTARD ON THE CAT

There's custard on the cat.
Why is there custard on the cat?
Did you put custard on the cat?

I don't know.

What do you mean, I don't know?
Did you put custard on the cat?

I might have.

You might have!
You might have!

It's just you and the cat here.
It's time to stop the tommyrot.
Did you put custard on the cat?

Yes.

Why? Why did you put custard on the cat?

Well, I wondered what a yellow cat would look like.

The child was curious.
The mother was furious.
The cat just said, Me-yell-ow.

SUMMER NIGHT ESCAPE

On those long ago
Summer evenings,
The children of New York
Dragged their mattresses
Onto the fire escape
In search of
A zephyr
Of cool air
And a chance to dream.

No air con back then,
Just a sweat box
Apartment.

So they crept through
Open windows
Buoyed by hope
Of finding relief
Slumbering
Above the street.

The boy sat
On the
Brooklyn Bridge
His feet were
In the water.

Longfellow

ABOUT THE AUTHOR

Alan j. Wright has been writing, performing, and promoting poetry all his life. He has always loved words and the marvelous ways in which they can be used to paint pictures in the mind of the reader.

This collection of adventurous verse for young poetry lovers builds upon Alan's previous book, *Searching for Hen's Teeth* and celebrates everything from pirates to pink pyjamas.

Alan wishes it to be known that he loves rhubarb, once ate nothing but tomato sandwiches in his school lunch for three years straight, accidentally set an emu on fire on a camping trip, sang with a band called This Way Out, and has never eaten snails.

I Bet There's No Broccoli on the Moon is a collection of Alan's poetry gathered from the far reaches of his experiences.

Printed in the United States
By Bookmasters